Bill and M

So glad to meet you -

New friends, nice!

David

Finding My Feet

DAVID C. STOLLER

RiverArts Press

New Hope, Pennsylvania

Photographs in this book were taken or provided by the author

Published by

RiverArts Press

973-919-4044 · dstol2636@gmail.com

Cover and title page painting: "Moby Dick" by Robert Beck

Page XV and page 146 quotes from "Song of the Open Road" by Walt Whitman

Page 47 and page 68 drawing: "Where Do I End, And You Begin?" by Mat Chivers

Layout design by Beth Schroeder

For My Parents,
Sidney and Billie Stoller,
Forever Young

Contents

ONE
To Keep Until I Die

3 .... Commandment
4 .... Cracks
5 .... Guff
6 .... The Unbearable Whiteness of Being
8 .... Why Do Cats Yowl?
9 .... On the All Gender Bathroom Line
10 .... A Harsh Wind
11 .... The Yellow Pot
12 .... Brittle the Night Sky
13 .... In the Dark
14 .... My Words
15 .... Eyes Closed
16 .... Her Habit of Life, to Learn
17 .... Leavening
18 .... You May Be Right
19 .... Life After *Game of Thrones*
20 .... Circling
21 .... Pursuit of Pleasure
22 .... And Sons
23 .... Then
24 .... God's Honest Truth
25 .... Hers
26 .... Fox Tale

Contents

27 .... Victim of Abuse
28 .... My Old Knee
29 .... One Lurch
30 .... Just Because
31 .... Death on the Terrace
32 .... The Wind Had Its Way
33 .... It
34 .... Rocky
35 .... My Old Catcher's Mitt
36 .... Reading 'Pickett's Charge'
37 .... Perchance to Dream
38 .... About Me
39 .... Alien
40 .... Not the Brightest Bulb
41 .... Suck It Up
42 .... For Bill
45 .... My Grandpa's Face

TWO

Rooted to This Soil

49 .... Nocturne For the Delaware
50 .... Diluvial Chat
51 .... Herons
52 .... "Teakettle, Teakettle, Teakettle"
53 .... A Hummingbird Hovered

Contents

54 .... Ashes to Ashes
55 .... Into the Pale Blue
56 .... We Will Build a Garden Here
57 .... First Morning in the Garden
58 .... Pity the Paw-Paw
59 .... Looking for Patterns
60 .... Suckers From the Understock
61 .... Returning Geese
62 .... Liaison Natural
63 .... Sundown
64 .... Tide In, Tide Out
65 .... Afternoon Swim
66 .... Peach Pit
67 .... Bird Call
69 .... Creation Myth

THREE

A Supplicant's Hands

73 .... The Wiring Doesn't Change
74 .... Pure Conversation
75 .... The King's Inner Grace
76 .... Note to Abe
77 .... Shpilkes
78 .... Rising Tide
79 .... Driving Down 32

Contents

80 .... Dreaming in Haikus
81 .... After Pound's "In a Station of the Metro"
82 .... Brancusi's Dog
83 .... Perhaps You're Thinking About Eternity
84 .... What Anchors Us
85 .... Our Philipsburg Bus
86 .... Everyday Moment
87 .... The Luckiest Man
88 .... Urban Olympics
89 .... End of the Wharf
90 .... Après Auden
91 .... While Cooking
92 .... Words Lose All Meaning
93 .... Fact or Fiction
94 .... Up Close
95 .... Cinnamon Bun
96 .... Old Wrench
97 .... Forget Recipes
98 .... Just a Dream
99 .... Algorithm
100 .... You're the Sea, Not The Waves: A Reed Sea Meditation
101 .... The Flow
102 .... Next Time
103 .... Something to Show For
104 .... Under the Closet Door

Contents

105 .... Narcissa
106 .... Morandi's Truth
107 .... The Seafarer
108 .... Without a Poem
111 .... Remington's Trapper

FOUR

Something That Was Mine

115 .... A Lifetime of Words
116 .... So Many
117 .... My Wonders
118 .... Once
119 .... Loss for Words
120 .... Our PIN
121 .... Sometimes
122 .... Sorrows
123 .... She
124 .... Sweet Dreams
125 .... Wouldn't It Be Nice
126 .... What We Shared
127 .... Longing

Contents

128 .... Mad for Clouds
129 .... The Sweet Lift of It
131 .... If I Could Make a Day

FIVE

Slow Time to Stone

135 .... Roadtrip
136 .... Footholds
137 .... Mirror Image
138 .... My Father Likes Words
139 .... A Mother's Touch
140 .... Billie and Sid, Two Old Trees
141 .... Lost
143 .... Our Isolation

Introduction

David Stoller is an exceptional poet. Like all artists, he can't not do it. There are too many important things to imagine, to create, to say. His poems examine subjects that matter to all of us in manifold degree. Their meanings are clear; sometimes delivered as gentle musings, sometimes as solid punches, always landed cleanly.

One of David's lines rattles in my head. "Show up anyway, you might even do some good." Well, here he is, and it's all good. Observing, caring, philosophizing, exploring. Ever in motion, in scrupulous verse. What a nice way to give, and to grasp.

–Robert Beck

Foreward

At the end of October, 2017, my father, Sid Stoller, then 93, suffered a heart attack that left him perilously weak. One month later, my wife Barbara had a serious fall that accelerated her dementia, leaving her, so accomplished and articulate, wholly without command of her words. I thought it very possible that either or both might be close to death, particularly my father, and decided to begin, in anticipation, studying and "practicing" "Kaddish," the Jewish mourning ritual that calls for the daily recitation of the Kaddish prayer for 11 months following the death of a parent or spouse. As I got into my "mourning" studies, a rabbi friend, alarmed, warned me to stop — "you're kaddishing your father to death". I followed his advice and decided instead to post a poem every day (which I did for well over a year) on Instagram ("The_Procreant_Urge"), dedicated to their healing. My father got to enjoy some of my poems (especially those about him) before he passed in October of last year, and Barbara remains one of my most loyal listeners. This book is dedicated to my father's memory, and my wife's continued well-being. And to my extraordinary mother, 94 and going strong. Here are some of those poems.

"Allons! The road is before us!
It is safe—I have tried it—my own feet have tried it well—
Be not detained!"

—Walt Whitman

ONE

"His tools, the box in which they lie,
For me **to keep until I die** —
and wear the mask that fits my head,
My grandpa's face"
—*from "My Grandpa's Face"*

Commandment

Forgive me, for I
Keep sinning effortlessly,
In my own image.

Seems I can't get past
One of those first Commandments —
No gods before me.

I make forms of clay
And each one is about me —
Models of myself.

Great expectations.
The latest reality.
My little golems.

I pinch their nostrils,
Take a breath, and blow ...

And they worship me.

Cracks

Sometime in my youth
I saw in a sidewalk's cracks
The face of my aged self.
A wearied old man passes;
I marvel at how well he looks.

Guff

He told me:
"Don't take any guff."
I nodded, wondering, what exactly was guff, anyway?

Perhaps it is the mayhem
that lurks on the edge
of pleasantries...
or the shadow that darkens
the underside of a wink...
or maybe it is the clotted
fat concealed in an
innocent slice of baloney.

The better advice
would have been to
keep my mouth shut.

The Unbearable Whiteness of Being

In the bright white glare,
I've been missing, in plain sight,
The boiling fury
Just below the worn mantle
Of past humiliations

Masked by a white noise
That has eased and protected
My peaceful slumber,
I've missed the whispered slurs,
The snap of lashed reminders

It's only when events
Are so shocking, so extreme
That I can't help but
See the crime through the glare,
Hear the clamor through the noise

That I will reach out
To my black friends and neighbors
And remind myself
That I am outraged, ashamed,
Committed to the struggle

But they are not fooled
I am not marked as they are
Indelibly black
Past, present, and permanent —
I'm only occasional

And claim as I might
That being marked once the same
By a yellow star
As fair game for brutality
Was qualifying somehow

I know it isn't
Could this be more bearable?
Would it matter more,
Were I to wear a black star
Pinned to my privileged whiteness?

Why Do Cats Yowl?

Why do cats yowl, that mournful cry —
ours last night
'til two-forty-five.

Limbo'd from bed,
grabbed my slippers and a light,
searching like Diogenes
for a feline in the night.

Looking for leads; what were her needs?
food, she was fed
sex, she was spayed
stress, hell, she slept all day...

I finally found Butterscotch,
by her last yowl,
in the laundry room,
asleep in a towel.

She was purring, her eyes were closed
happy she was as fresh-folded clothes.

On the All Gender Bathroom Line

'When we were kings'
Drumming through my mind...
I found myself thinking
How to sensibly address
The use of pronouns in general text

Still pre-dominant is "he"
Of course
Generalized as "Man"
In most discourse

But surely "she"
So dispossessed
Is equally awkward
Put to press

And stirring through
The equities
Is the straw called gender identity...
"Wake up, man"

There's the two-minute call
And this damn line hasn't moved
At all
O, I knew come this day would —
Welcome to the Sisterhood!

A Harsh Wind

A harsh wind blew hard
like to blow this house the hell
into the next yard
ranting windows wailing cuffed
no pillow could stuff
pushing past the jambs I see
spent uprooted trees
toppled out of soil soaked soft
brittled limbs now lost

All once more is threshed and clean
Harsh wind – blow through me!

The Yellow Pot

The yellow pot, safe
If emptied and stored, is cracked —
A simple trust breached.
The snow fills its crooked smile
And the fault around my heart.

Brittle the Night Sky

Brittle the night sky.
All could collapse with a cough.
I hear my breath
A freight whistle light years past,
The rumble of a long haul.

In the Dark

Quiet drapes the house
I can't sleep and slip downstairs
To my favorite chair.
I sit, eyes closed, and wonder
What I might learn in the dark.

My Words

It's late, a blank page;
I look outside for the moon,
Reliable muse,
But she's dancing somewhere else,
Singing to another my words.

Eyes Closed

A battered guard rail
Was all that stood between me
And the world to come.

Her Habit of Life, To Learn

Her gift, an old book,
Had no title, its pages worn,
Underscored, folded...
It was her habit of life,
To learn, now held in my trust.

Leavening

I watched an old man
Reach skyward, up on his toes:
'Let us be leavened'
I imagined him saying...
Yes, rising above it all.

You May Be Right

In my current state
I tend to accommodate —
Mencken made the case:
Loved or scorned for what he'd write,
Answered each: "You may be right."

Life After *Game of Thrones*

What about these shows
We take so seriously,
All this fire and blood...
Leave me alone with my books —
Oh, and "*Grey's Anatomy.*"

Circling

A pregnant mother
Rubs circles on her belly
And seems comforted.
I rub round my swollen knee
And feel the spread of relief.

Pursuit of Pleasure

My cat has a view—
She's an epicurean.
I'm studying her
Pursuit of pleasure, *Id est*,
Being rubbed the right way.

And Sons

I walked through the old downtown,
Boarded beyond possibilities,
rust claiming its promises.

A sign, hanging by
a single, desolated hinge,
offered only a faded legacy:
"And Sons."

Then

I tried to embrace
Winter's undisputed charms —
Then the car wouldn't start.

God's Honest Truth

A fortune cookie,
of all things,
Revealed God's honest truth:
"Life is Holy — Celebrate it!"
Could there be a better proof?

Hers

She tugged so slightly
'Til the white-tipped, earth-sweet spear
Was hers to nibble.

Fox Tale

The fox cocked her head —
God she was so beautiful.
She has a question...
Then with a swish she turned tail.
"The answer's in the lyric,"
I called after her...
But she'd left me with the blues.

Victim of Abuse

My knee, on death row,
Final appeals exhausted,
Swollen with remorse
Confirmed incorrigible,
Will be replaced tomorrow.

My Old Knee

My grandson Eddie
Asked a question kids would ask:
Where is your old knee?
Don't know, said I — felt a pang...
My old knee deserved better.

One Lurch

A cross-country flight —
Hell on newly-replaced knees
and the fools they serve;
Down and back that aisle I drilled,
One lurch from catastrophe.

Just Because

Just because he said
'May I offer you my seat'
I rose to my height,
The doors opened, and I left —
Slouching towards seventy.

Death on the Terrace

The bird lay still, dead.
Why the surprise when things die?
I looked more closely —
Wings settled in classic repose,
Death's austere beauty.

The Wind Had Its Way

I hugged my good luck:
All was perfectly ordered,
Designed to matter,
Until the wind had its way
And all was scatter, scatter.

It

On the edge of sleep
I tried to hold Consciousness —
but slipped out of It.

Rocky

Caught the masked bandit
Picking through the emptied can —
Fiendish little hands.
Turned to stare while fleecing there...
Then sauntered off, not a care.

My Old Catcher's Mitt

Webbing frayed, thumb split,
Same sweet spot I rubbed my spit—
My old catcher's mitt.
Whiff of neatsfoot fills my nose,
I pound the pocket, eyes closed.

Reading 'Pickett's Charge'

Death was on their lips.
I know my heart's bitter taste,
So well acquired.
Boldly marked in today's book:
'Each man fights on his own hook.'

Perchance to Dream

I nap anywhere —
A dentist's lead vest kills me;
In rehab today,
I finished a tough session
Waving to adoring crowds.

About Me

I open my mouth
And it sounds too familiar;
I extend a hand
And my shadow's reaching first...
Can't I get away from me?

Alien

The subway doors closed.
An arm snaked through, hand grasping—
Frozen, we all stared.
Just as suddenly, the arm...
Withdrew, and we shrugged ahead.

Not the Brightest Bulb

I stood on the stool
Straining to unscrew the bulb.
The thing wouldn't budge.
The pathos of a back-flip
Impressed me, and I stood down.

Suck It Up

My biggest regrets
Are the times that I held back.
Shy or self-conscious?
Who cares — speak up anyway.
You might even do some good.

For Bill

A kind man is sick
We missed the signs of peril
How did we not know
That such a sweet, gentle soul
Was away so long at war.

My Grandpa's Face

My grandpa's face, I saw, now dead,
The ragged breaths at last had fled,
Skin drawn tight over cheekbones high,
Jaw set square to a practiced eye,
Stone-faced he stares from sheeted bed.

By saw and mallet he was bred,
A ripped and cross-cut life he led,
A map of mitred cuts there lie,
My grandpa's face.

From chin to brow I traced the thread,
Feeling for something left unsaid —
His tools, the box in which they lie,
For me to keep until I die —
And wear the mask that fits my head,
My grandpa's face.

TWO

“I am **rooted to this soil**.
Born of a seed
carried across ancient seas
in the craw
of the brave swallow
urged in perfect time
to return home, ...”
—*from “Creation Myth”*

Nocturne For the Delaware

The day has quieted.
The river,
released from all apprehensions,
eases.

Movement below,
so richly imagined in daylight,
passes

beneath the dark glassine veil
that unspools slowly
between shadowed flanks
following its own soft swell
to the sea.

Diluvial Chat

Diluvial chat,
overheard in the birdsong:
Waters gathering.

Herons

Shoreline Pharisees,
Each dreaming with open eyes
About Ancient floods

"Teakettle, Teakettle, Teakettle"

Our Carolina wrens,
do you know their cry?
Even more piercing
with babies nearby:
"Teakettle, Teakettle, Teakettle!"

In the begonias
there's where she settled
Hailed their arrival
proving her mettle:
"Teakettle, Teakettle, Teakettle!"

They build their nest
with purloined scatter
We try not to watch
as if it's no matter
"Teakettle, Teakettle, Teakettle!"

And sometime soon
a brood we'll see
To take up the tune
quite naturally:
"Teakettle, Teakettle, Teakettle!"

A Hummingbird Hovered

A hummingbird hovered
before my nose,
fixed me with his gaze;
I followed the arc
in which he rose –
and vanished in the haze.

Was he a sense
before the touch,
an idea that tipped the tongue,
or a song so lovely
and so real
still unwritten, still unsung.

Ashes to Ashes

(Sung to "Ring Around the Rosie")

See the Emerald Borer
Alien Marauder
Ash trees, ash trees
All fall down

Larval tubers chew the bark
Suck the sap until it's dark
Ash trees, ash trees
All fall down

Brittled broken crowns are grey
Mottled leaves just fall away
Ash trees, ash trees
All fall down

Fading rings round mortal wood
Stumps abound where forests stood
Ashes, Ashes
All. Fall. Down.

Into the Pale Blue

Pale blue lay the egg,
Beneath the broad cedar spread —
I searched above, whose?

Such a prize to lose,
So beautifully whole, still,
After such a spill.

What if it was placed
As a simple act of grace —
I looked around, whom?

Incipient bloom,
A perfection of the form,
Aspired to, unborn ....

Or perhaps a sign,
From a friend who'd crossed the line —
Of the world to come?
Who years ago, near death, said:
"Find me by a pale blue egg".

We Will Build A Garden Here

We will build a garden here
of dappled light and graveled paths
with native plants and natural craft
bordered by the Delaware.

We will build a garden here
of measured growth and cycled time
with disparate elements all aligned
such deeper truths that might appear.

We will build a garden here
practice the art of setting stone
embrace the wild as our own
come to our senses present and clear.

First Morning in the Garden

Daybreak pushed
through the gray mist
that draped the river.

Old stones
set in new marks
warmed to their task,
Amused by the young trees,
seedlings barely rooted,
fluttering between hopeful breaths.

All smelled like dirt
And it was good.
The first day.

Pity the Paw-Paw

Fruit of the obscure
Dissed in its own climate zone
Pity the Paw-Paw
Once toast of the Delawares
It's time to bring the brand back.

Looking for Patterns

River in twilight,
Geometries are at work.
Looking for patterns,
I get lost in the shadows,
And spiral to the bottom.

Suckers From the Understock

When I feel threatened
Our Ginkgo provides refuge
Longest-lived of trees
Survivor of Hiroshima
This ancient tree is my strength.

But usurpers come —
Suckers from the understock
Surround the trunk...
unchecked, they will kill our tree.
Well, they were checked, and checked good.

Returning Geese

How sweet to reclaim,
After so hard a journey.
A place of one's own.

Imagine our pride
When this Canadian pair
Nested at our home.

And since then we've seen
Twenty years of gosling broods
Gaggling on our lawn.

So sad to report
This year's steep fall from favor —
For their nesting domicile...
They chose our neighbor.

Liaison Natural

The warming river
Has waited all evening long
For the rain's soft touch.
They embrace, veiled like lovers —
Stealing a kiss, clothed in mist.

Sundown

Freefalling seaward,
The sun fled the horizon
— Slash of crimson wake —
That it could ever escape
Dying again and again.

Tide In, Tide Out

Tide in
Tide out
A day's record
Strewn about.

Tangled masses
Empty shells
All erased
By evening's swell.

Ere we sleep
Review the day:
words and pictures —
which will stay?

Memory's tide
Drained by sleep;
Sift the debris
From what to keep.

See, from its midst,
Your life as a tale,
with chapters yet to tell;
Maybe then you'll enjoy it more,
And more likely
Live it well.

Afternoon Swim

From our shore across,
the doe with intention swims;
impelled by nature —
or just following a whim?

Peach Pit

Stone seed of the fruit
Whorled as the fuzzed face is smooth
Happy the peach pit.

Bird Call

We twelve-year-old molts
Had our own call: "Fuckin' A!"
Crowed with two thumbs up.

Creation Myth

I am rooted to this soil.
Born of a seed
carried across ancient seas
in the craw
of the brave swallow
urged in perfect time
to return home,
and dropped from the sky
into which I stare
spreading my wings.

THREE

"And see how gently
he holds the reins, open and soft—
a supplicant's hands
once crabbed in the raw grip
of a land harsh and wild"
—*from "Remington's Trapper"*

The Wiring Doesn't Change

Catch yourself wondering, why it is,
You've turned out This or That?
Can one pivot to another self,
like an acrobat?

Sad to say, but character's fixed,
Personality stays the same;
no matter what the twists and turns,
the wiring doesn't change.

Are you high stakes, or small change?
Inclined to blame, or take the pain?
Prefer the sacred or profane? ...
The wiring doesn't change.

What tastes good, and what feels right,
When you run and when you fight,
play the game with all your might —
The wiring doesn't change.

So here's the deal: own your life —
stake and defend your claim.
Do your best, and bless the rest.
The wiring doesn't change.

Pure Conversation

The Taoists believed
That pure conversation led
To enlightenment...
Provided, a weeping tree
And a moss-soft riverbank.

The King's Inner Grace

Muhammad Ali
Saw compassion's face and cried —
The 'king's' inner grace.
See those who would be king
Cry, and little children die.

Note to Abe

You must be brooding:
Your house is so divided,
malice is everywhere;
our better angels have fled.

We do recall that
mournful epitaph:
"Now he belongs to the ages"

Well, searching through those
mystic chords of memory,
we found a blood-stained
claim check, long lost
in your marbled words...
Here it is. Please come back. Now.

Shpilkes*

Shpilkes are these little beasts
crawling up your spine —
make you jump up from your seat
if they begin to climb

I think, perhaps, it's nature's way
to say enough's enough
time to get up and move around —
those shpilkes can get rough

Don't take it personal
if it's your guest, afflicted
by the insidious pest —

The shpilkes got him,
nothing to say,
he'll be back another day.

**Yiddish for impatience, agitation. Not reserved only for Jewish people.*

Rising Tide

Tide of human flow,
Washing up against closed doors;
Is the rising tide
The one promised to lift all —
Or the one in which we drown?

Driving Down 32

Grey-flinted hillside
Sloped forty-five to the road
Rich with detritus —
Orphaned stumps and timbered bones.
We age like seasoned hillsides.

Dreaming in Haikus

He emptied himself
Looking for a sure way in
And was hardly missed

Loss can be too fresh
He felt nothing but empty
Save the date for grief

Man slips on a peel
Why am I laughing like this
I couldn't help it

Show me a good gasp
Chorused across a filled room —
A raw truth laid bare

In truth, people lie
Omission or commission
Tell me it's not so.

After Pound's "In a Station of the Metro"

The apparition
of these hollow-eyed faces

Rotted blooms hanging
On a long stalk scorched

Brancusi's Dog

Constantino, sitting with his
snow-white, long-haired Polar,
muses on the hidden, inner reality
of his furred friend.

Eyes that light up in greeting,
mourn departure, flash in defense,
should be highlighted —
Let's make what's intrinsic unmistakable.

Nose and mouth (tongue!) sweet,
wet, warm, leading, longing, loving,
should claim a more elegant length,
befitting such clarity of purpose.

And character, that revels in being
common, all sniffed and sniffing,
none better or worse. Short-coated,
black and white. Balanced and fair.

A great calm settles over Constantino.
Such a feeling
a dog delivers,
or a design reduced to its essence.

Perhaps You're Thinking About Eternity

I

Sweep of a hand
Slips into shadows
By whose command
Becomes the night.

II

Slips into shadows
An instant, in passing,
Becomes the night
Eclipsing the future.

III

An instant in passing
Betrays not its secret
Eclipsing the future
In every day moments.

IV

Betrays not its secret
of awful Significance
In every day moments,
Leaf after leaf.

V

Of awful significance
Impulse to ruin
Leaf after leaf
Down to the root.

VI

Impulse to ruin
Mad to discover
Down to the root
What epoch is this?

VII

Mad to discover
The fractions of waking
What epoch is this.
Poised on cataclysm.

VIII

The fractions of waking
Sweep of a hand
Poised on cataclysm
By whose command.

What Anchors Us

The rusted anchor
Rose by half from the ruin
Of the crumbled homestead;
Remnant of an inland sea
Or a world blown off course?

Our Phillipsburg Bus

Our Phillipsburg bus —
The local two-dollar ride
Lurched through fraught ascent
Behind a brooding mixer
And its slow-spinning cement.

Everyday Moment

You might turn around,
Catch an everyday moment,
Hold it very close.
Turn it, turn it again, and —
Find eternity in it.

The Luckiest Man

sun, soil, open sky
Two trees planted, side by side
One lives and one dies.

His name suffices, "Lou Gehrig's Disease"
The Yankees 'Iron Horse'
Pulled his draft through sixteen seasons
Every day, as a matter of course.

And then a tremble, a tremor, a wave,
A grip suddenly weak;
Doomed, a man no one could save,
Drowning on his feet.

A legacy resting, as much or more
On a perfect body disabled —
Than on his exploits, the stuff of lore,
That same body enabled.

No simpler grace was ever known,
facing his grieving fans:
He thanked them all for the kindness shown
To him, "The Luckiest Man."

Urban Olympics

Let us praise the one
Who squeezes through subway doors
spilling not a drop.

End of the Wharf

Farewells made, he shrugs
against a chill he now feels.
What was it she said?
A paper scrap — a note, perhaps —
drifts past, turns, and vanishes.

Après Auden

Do we not have a
peculiar opacity
about things like roofs?
We don't really notice them
until our own needs repair.

While Cooking

Tears fell in the pot,
Seasoning a memory,
stirred and tasted, served.

Words Lose All Meaning

Words lose all meaning
dissolved in blood-soaked school-yards
neutered by official condolences
glazed by grief-counselors
deafened, drowned out, by
GUNFIRE

A child asks, "Why?"
And we can only answer:
Because —
we have failed you
we have lost our bearings
we refuse, we deny, we ignore
our responsibility
and because
those lost are not our own —
until they are.

Fact or Fiction

We all have a past,
A crossroads of many minds —
Which version is right?
Formed we are by memories,
Lost the same in our fictions.

Up Close

See a thing so close
That its truth comes alive —
The story it tells
The thought that shapes its meaning
The desire that says its name.

Cinnamon Bun

There's 'pleasure in things,'
Nature seems to enjoy swirls.
Take the cinnamon bun —
DaVinci would have relished
The sweet at its core, uncoiled.

Old Wrench

The snake-twisted form
Of the two-headed wrench
Is the pure expression
Of humanity
And intellect, merged.

Forget Recipes

Forget recipes
Or empty forms of guidance.
Only readiness:
Embrace that which is nearest,
Proceed as the way opens.

Just a Dream

What a great relief
To wake up and realize
That the person you killed
and dismembered is still alive
and none the wiser for it.

Algorithm

Where is the real world—
O soulful algorithm...
What is left to learn?

You're The Sea, Not The Waves: A Reed Sea Meditation

Wave after wave
Reed-soaked sea
Rolling the length of your fears

Turn and face them
You're the sea not the waves
Savor the salt of your tears

The waves are your doorway
Your refuge your strength
The multitude that you are

Pass through the waters
Gathered beside you
You'll see that it wasn't so far

The Flow

The flow belies a turbulence,
opposing forces merge,
nature might incline towards balance
but its paths diverge.

Cataclysm roils the world,
from whence new forms emerge;
as clouds, or waves, or spirals curled —
it's that old procreant urge.

Tectonic plates can't keep still,
They're all about the surge;
what we fear as upheaval —
just a world that's on the verge.

What seems so random, isn't so —
foretold in primordial bath;
think you really go with the flow?
It's all about the math.

Next Time

It was good he said
And smelled the river close.
Yes she rubbed his feet.
They dreamed of their younger days.
And next time will be better.

Something to Show For

At the very least,
a fine sense of loss offers
something to show for.

Under the Closet Door

So neatly ordered
A wardrobe of observance:
Joy and heartbreak wait
Under the closet door

Narcissa

She squats at the edge
Trying to find her image
In the dark water.

A touch, so soft, as she might
Caress her own mirrored face.

Morandi's Truth

Pity the artist:
There is nothing more abstract
Than reality

The Seafarer

The red-rimmed old squint
Watched the slow movement of whales
Span the bitter blue sky

Without a Poem

Without a poem
A day should never end.

Without a poem,
A broken heart won't mend.

Without a poem
A man ain't got a friend.

Remington's Trapper

Remington's trapper,
so curiously smooth-faced
considering all
domestic imperatives
shaving would seem to require.

And see how gently
he holds the reins, open and soft –
a supplicant's hands
once crabbed in the raw grip
of a land so harsh and wild.

FIVE

"I would take all that was offered
and make **something that was mine**
and I would distill every sensation
to a truth I could speak
and I would listen to my desire
say my name."

—*from "If I Could Make a Day"*

A Lifetime of Words

A lifetime of words,
few now spoken,
and those half-drawn,
bundled, broken.
Mustered soldiers,
Wearied command,
left to molder
where they stand.
Sometimes flushed,
burst out loud;
sometimes drizzled,
misted cloud.
Yet somewhere —
all those words make sense.
fully formed in present tense;
uttered once, forever fair,
none are lost, all are there.

So Many

"You are so many,"
she murmured, still half-asleep;
"I only want one."

My Wonders

We heard geese overhead.

She got up, peered through
the blinds.

"Who took my wonders?"

Once

"Read it once again,"
her eyes filled, remembering
a place, a voice, once.

Loss for Words

We are at a loss
for words that are between us,
braided once now loosed.

A tongue that recalled
a lyric with precision
and toasted excuses,

Strains to simply say
the ordinary things in
ordinary ways.

Fitting puzzle pieces
looking for edges, corners
to find our way in,

Or a riverstone
to rub, with incantations
for its narration;

Perhaps we'll summon
with kabalistic fervor
sages to translate,

Like the penitent,
reciting the alphabet,
God to form the prayer.

Still, there's what to say...
We watch for ships, and when there's not—
Then we'll sail away.

Our PIN

She woke with a start,
from someplace, lost: "Where are we?"
"Here," I said. "Home."
She stared, unconvinced.
I remembered, then, our PIN:
Hands — three slow squeezes.
Confirmed. She curled, back.

Sometimes

Sometimes it just rains,
inside and out,
through a crack
we can't bind or seal
that swells and widens
until we are breached.

Sorrows

Only some suffer?
No, we all have our sorrows;
my pillow knows mine.

She

She who could tear bark from a tree
with the flash of her tongue
Who could summon a Sondheim lyric
with the toss of her head

Who could crisply argue the irrefutable
logic of common sense...
has lost command of her words, which
sometimes explode like grouse flushed

or flash like stirred embers, or
puddle and evaporate,
only to be returned as
raindrops, or drizzle, or fog.

And sometimes they are clear and
insistent, but insensible to us.
We listen closely, consider context,
measure inflection, weigh emphasis,
reach for the spirit if not the letters

and the patience to stay in place...
hoping that all those words
are somewhere ordered, collated,
bundled, ready to recall.

Sweet Dreams

My sweet girl, asleep
Glasses pressed to a turned cheek
I lift them just so –
Her eyes open, close again
I kiss her forehead
She smiles, forty years ago.

Wouldn't It Be Nice

Woke up to sunshine
And an old favorite song
"Wouldn't It Be Nice."
She rose, twirled, arms overhead
And we danced like it sure would.

What We Shared

The hawk arced slowly
Against the gold-setting sky.
We followed its length.
She nudged me, a red tail, right?
Yes I pulled her close, bursting.

Longing

Of loss and longing —
the worst is not belonging.
How convenient if one's tears
Were the answer to such fears.

Mad for Clouds

Mad for clouds, she searched
For the coded narrative
That would change her life

The Sweet Lift of It

She imagined flight:
Ties loosened, ballast released;
The sweet lift of it.

If I Could Make a Day

If I could make a day
She would say
It would be a day like today
of color and geometry
and river rippled sunlight
and birdsong's call and response
And what would you take
from this day
I would take all that was offered
and make something that was mine
and I would distill every sensation
to a truth I could speak
and I would listen to my desire
say my name

FIVE

Three generations,
suffered in isolation,
too late for repair,
Their secrets and mysteries
hardened in **slow time to stone**."

—*from "Our Isolation, Part I"*

Roadtrip

Dad no longer drives
His garage filled with longing
For one more roadtrip
To find what he thought he dreamed
With a map of words and names

Footholds

Dad is climbing
down
Feeling around
for footholds
Once struck climbing
up.

Mirror Image

Mirror, five A.M.
Looking at me/my father:
same face, same regret.

My Father Likes Words

My father likes words,
'Factotum' a favorite,
When 'fulsome' is misused he broods,
And gimmie a buck
Everytime something "sucks"
He scowls when it's used.

I pity this poor man,
This prophet scorned,
Trapped in our miasmic scrabble -
For whom 'coherence'
Is the 'Sine Qua Non'...
Railing at the towering babble.

And still he believes, to what effect,
In the gods of Clear, Concise, and Correct.

A Mother's Touch

My mother used a blackened pin
for splinter extrication
Warning that to leave it in
risked cardiac penetration.

We always yielded to her touch
deft, in the circumstance
Better than bearing the heavy hand
of my father and his lance.

And without fail, the insurgent gone,
the poor finger quickly mended;
All apprehension of a poisoned heart
just as quickly ended.

We still get splinters, deeper now
and hard to tell apart
And just as surely, left untended,
they will slowly pierce the heart.

Billie and Sid, Two Old Trees

The storm, so fierce,
now fully spent;
clean air, and sweet release.

Amidst the scatter,
beside a bench,
sat our two old trees.

How to explain,
all others shorn,
yet these had their leaves?

The landscape bare,
How still adorned;
which gods did they appease?

Ovid's Baucis
and Philemon,
by Zeus and Xerces spared,
had only some bread,
a little wine,
and this they freely shared.

Their reward, a wish
granted to each —
to last eternally:
when one is called,
take the other, too —
Let us live as two old trees.

Lost

I cover my eyes,
Hear the clamor of Yiddish
From a million tongues...
The towns and markets are there;
The Jews, it seems, never were.

Our Isolation

I.

The catastrophe.
Our family's great sadness.
A stone that covers
Things over but not ended,
That come inside us and live.

Three generations
Suffered in isolation.
Too late for repair,
Their secrets and mysteries
Hardened in slow time to stone.

Here is what I know:
David, my great grandfather,
Carpenter by trade,
A pious man, I gathered
From a scribbled notation.

'From Grodetz' it says
On the deportation list.
I have a picture —
He looks sturdy. I wonder
If he tangled with cossacks.

What else do I know?
He and my great grandmother
Hid from the Nazis
For three years then were betrayed
And murdered at Birkenau.

II.

Three years of silence,
Of whispered encouragement,
Of unspoken dread,
Of Torah, prayer, psalms, ritual,
Of remembering their lives.

Across the ocean,
My grandpa Jack, oldest son,
Hears only silence,
From voices hidden or dead,
Shuttered in his sorrow.

Did he say kaddish?
Did it relieve the stone's weight,
Heavy as the tools
He carried to work each day,
And left to me in his trust?

I see my father
Bent to his work, chin in hand,
Writing and rewriting
Drafts in painstaking yiddish
Of letters to his Zayde.

Such correspondence
Continued for years, I'm told,
Until it ended.
He ground his teeth forever.
Not a word of those letters.

III.

Three generations
Carried their isolation
One to the other,
Their secrets and mysteries
Hardened in slow time to stone.

The stone is mine now.
It is a gift with a price:
'Accept me', it says,
And take all of the living,
Things ended and beginning.

Their stone no longer,
Let them be freed from its hold.
Something has ended,
And something begins and grows,
With its own labors and joys.

"Camerado, I give you my hand!
I give you my love more precious than money,
I give you myself before preaching or law;
Will you give me yourself? Will you come travel with me?
Shall we stick by each other as long as we live?"

—Walt Whitman

author, age 5

Made in the USA
Middletown, DE
29 September 2020

20502378R00097